A Garden for Black Boys

Between the Stages of Soil and Stardust

W.J. LOFTON

Author's note

this collection of poetry is an interrogation and an answering of humanity. page by page, this work provides a home for black men. black women. for those who see our plight and seek to understand it. this is an invitation to peer through windows: an act of radical love displaying black bodies as whole and beautiful. as i draw back the curtains i am compelled by the words of the undeniable, Audre Lorde, "I am deliberate and afraid of nothing". recurrently in society, there are no spaces in which black men and women can fully express themselves, either being labeled as too angry, having too much attitude and even being tagged as weak within their own hood for *feeling* and *being* alive. we exist within a culture where police are weaponized against people of color. we are snatched from spaces because people *feel* as though we do not belong or should not have the access to them. each poem provides this safe space; a shelter purposed to provide opportunities to freely mourn, fellowship, and celebrate the experiences of black folk. the poems do not tread lightly when taking on an armada of serious issues such as class, equality, equity, race, gender, disability, sexuality and most importantly, the right to live the human experience as authentically possible. there is an aching and a healing to be found. here, black men can define themselves, to live fully between the stages of soil and stardust (from beginning of life to end). the adumbration of hypermasculinity is stripped of its power to emasculate the very men it is meant to empower. here, black women are visible and are not reduced by the patriarchal gaze. black women are the birthers of culture and continue to be our moral compass. as much as i would like to say this was a selfless laboring, i cannot. as much as these poems are for you, the reader, they are for me. the past few years i have fought to find words that accurately describe the loss i feel every time i see a fresh corpse thrown in front of social media and the news. i know there are many more vanishing bodies that go undocumented. these murders come raging on the winds of fear and exalted hatred that thrives on racism. girls who look like my sisters, boys who look like me. they could have easily passed as members of my family. unlike some who have unfortunately become desensitized to the onslaught, my soul aches with each black body unjustly and disproportionately claimed. i imagine Emmett Till being beaten with the flashlight that would eventually render him unconscious, his fourteen-year-old body being wrapped in barbed wire, a bullet piercing his skull and vanquishing any vestige of hope or dream he dared to hold as his. what sort of mock crucifixion is this? my mind visits Amadou Diallo and how forty-one bullets were fired by police, triturating his body. with each murder my stomach turns, i mourn in silence, the anger sets in, i write toward a distant sanity. there becomes a constant roll call that leaves me emptier than the first time i rehearsed it : *Trayvon Martin, Oscar Grant, Michael Brown, Clifford Glover, Jordan Davis, Tamir Rice, Sandra Bland, Addie Mae Collins, Cynthia Wesley, Carole Roberts, Carol Denise McNair, Sean Bell, Rekia Boyd, Eric Garner, Stephon Clark, Ramarley Graham, John Crawford III, Aiyana Jones, Alton Sterling, Laquan McDonald, Walter Scott, Philando Castile, Renisha McBride* and the names continue and loop themselves into an endless song. a song that shakes me and forces me to question the miracle of Chance the Rapper's opening lyric in Chuck English's *Glam*, where he belts the chords, *"God loves all my niggas"*. negus'. when hopelessness found me, i was forced to find a truth that would anchor me. and so i dreamed. i began to imagine a place where graves where void of slaughtered black bodies, no matter if they arrived there due to police brutality or as victim of their own environment. i dared to dream. my mind grasped for traces of life and hope. there had to be a place where sorrow shook into light. instead of a grave, a garden emerged. out from behind the veil of despair, black bodies surfaced from the soil. a home of resurrection was created. These poems are not only about the loss of black bodies but the loss of innocence, friendships, safety, and the ownership to one's body. i know that silence is complicit, and it dishonors the soul. this is my breaking up of the quiet. this is my rock through the glass window. it is my eternal wish to be free without the metronome of having to explain why black life matters-why my life matters-why my siblings'-my goddaughter-my loved ones' lives matter. america may never lend an apology to the brown and black bodies that anguished from the Atlantic Slave Trade to *here*. however, it will hear what we have to say about our pain, our joy, our murder, our healing, and this constant assault on our brothers and sisters. we too, deserve a space where our laughs can blossom, and our mothers do not have to bury us, a garden where we can grow, rooted in loving soil until the heavens will have us. i honor my ancestors who stood on auction blocks; the ones who prayed and fought and fought and prayed. I honor the Harriet Tubmans and the Nat Turners who called out into the night to *steal away, steal away, steal away to Jesus.* i am hopeful with this confrontation of pain, this work joins in with the voices of change. maybe not a rock through the glass ceiling but a stone for the window.

for my siblings Ricky, Reggie, Chris, Willie, Willette, and Jeanine and everything in which you've had to bear. i love you endlessly.

for Emmett Till and the black boys before and after him.

*for every black girl that has gone **missing,** in every sense of the word.*

for the damaged and the healing. the pain only affirms the growth.

table of contents

"As they were going out, they met a man from Cyrene, named Simon, and forced him to carry the cross."

Matthew 27:32

Jesus called in a loud voice, "Lazarus, come out!". The dead man came out, his hands and feet wrapped with strips of linen, and a cloth around his face. Jesus said to them, "Take off the grave clothes and let him go."

John 11:43

"To be sensual, I think, is to respect and rejoice in the force of life, of life itself, and to be present in all that one does, from the effort of loving to making of bread"- James Baldwin

"I made my shame move out because it wasn't paying rent to my bones."- Jamillah Bell

triptych:

carpeted   floor   seventy-inch   television   three knights
spitting sun
playing the Dozens be praxis for
heirs to kingless men
syrup sloshing inside cups softens even the hardest of soil
sides of these black sons they aint ever shown another
black   man   yielding blossoms, bunglingly

honest with sleeves up
wounds weeping and bleeding
nameless bruises
burning to release his brother

with either bullet   forgiveness   or sharing a blunt
ablaze

seems like every corner   corporate office   and *or*
street curb be waiting
to snatch his snapback like the prison always seems to
snatch his daddy back
to exorcise dream from his ankles
excommunicate the Lord from his house
rebuke any angel or praying grandmother that may attempt
to love his shatter into some   redeemable sonnet   some
endless fantasy where being black is synonymous with
immortality

where Chicago aint a warzone   but nickname for
Wakanda
the cups lick themselves empty
the emptiness sloshes up from   their throats   spills from
their lips

slowly, they begin to understand the demands of
forgiveness while being fatherless

maybe it's a rap   or a hymn
however, the prayer draws back   the curtain   *they must
mean it.*

dancing on the moon:

shirt silhouetted over my head   eclipsing the sight of
living room to blind joy ride my body   a nebula alive
with the shouting dance, of the pentecostal folks spinning
as so many black   boys do   outta control

carpet unfolding into dance floor five-year-old feet armed
in battle, the language of twists   and turns natural --- my
mother was a runaway woman, passing along the ancient
art of slipping from one place to another, quietly

from dance to the bow the encore – the sharp skirt of glass
table pulling my eyelid into flash pain

moon passing over the trim of my   father's voice son be
held by percussive pang then father's arms turning darkness
into day

a knight wounding those invisible gangsters responsible for
his son's fall

god whispers him up from that grief:

god whispers him up from that grief/subpoenaed black boy
by his Nile River navel from

depression's mouth/ the cold adulation that arrived when
your eyes were closed/ slipped

underneath the bedsheets, held fast to the night of your
flesh/ god whispered him away from

that ghetto sadness/ brown skin curling up from the
darkness/ spine dancing like

chrysanthemum petals finding their legs in winter/ slow but
deliberate breathing/ joy surely

comes this morning/ brown boy stop allowing tears to
know the lines of your face/ black boy

needs to know he can be alone and not die because of it/ he
has been running with nothing to

escape from/eventually the petals touch/the soul runs into
the flesh-itself

goods instead of men, graves in place of gardens:

if there is smoke
then there must be some *thing*   some *body*
burning

some black boy who has lent his bones to some street fire
turned shooting
turned his mother from widower to nothing
for what do you call a woman who loses her child
what decorated frame do you place her tears
turned white-american satire

a giggle gone godless   a hijacked joke draped between
the lines of the second amendment
traipsed into a traitorous house looking for humanity and
humanity's God

list the black girls
who never laid their backs against the gurney of hashtags
recite their souls
trace your teeth over their ghosts
how quick they become ghouls
taste how history always makes the black woman

a haunting,

too heavy of a goddess to pray to or for
damned her joy into a pearl coffin
flipped her over and asked her for ass and assets

left her with absence
presented crumbs, made folly the golden crown
and we wonder why the earth's sobs sound so familiar
the same chorus our mother's smile sung when it went all
mystery on us
left us a bouquet of clouds
and a hope as wet as tears

when the saints go marching they bring their sisters:

how many scars can fall onto the backdrop

of a black girl's skin

making her tough,

walking with all that big bang in her chest

expectations on zero gravity

after being let down

again, and again

i know more women who remind me of Tupac

rather than the men sharing the same skin

and nose ring as him

my sister is a

five

foot

four,

compendium on revolution

an alleyway for the homeless

a summer of sunday mornings

for souls in search of a song

she is Lauryn after the Fugees

post-Beyoncé

when learning to black girl magic her

lemons

into lemonade

a Viola Davis type of sun ray

no fence has enough wood or wire to become her prison

my sister

has dissolved sorrow

birthed Kool-Aid smile in its wake

shaken the earth with her prayers

her spine be miracle

all those tears be wonder

how many stars dim to the light of her eye

sky cracks its lips to laugh

sun bows

moonlight buckles its grace

when black girl swallows and own the scars

that she never asked for

black girl

pops gum

twists hair

got degree

for her

i would turn an army of goons into ghosts

deadbeats into dust

because she has loved her brother into panther, through
pain

for Briunca's brother and the other brothers out there:

you get no grieving days for cousins
the earth snatches a brother   a sister   a name plated in
gold or silver
someone else identified my brother's body last night
before i ever had the chance to pray

that the gunshot didn't carry his smile away
tied his spine into a wishbone
twisted his name into a dancing wisp of smoke
a gasping breath trying to sing   a song that he no longer
knows the words to

a prayer looking for some god to bestow his bones to
the light reminds me of your absence
knowing that we must bury your body inside the earth
away from my tears
tomorrow, we must give you yellow roses as if that is all
you   deserve   body being a soulless vase

for the lord is my shepherd and dear God i find myself in
want
for this grief has an entire playlist and my name is on every
damn track
this anger is shaking to get naked
to wash itself down in some good old-fashioned healing
pass the lemon balm, spread it over the left isle of your
chest

you aint here
it just aint right
i call your phone, it rings   and rings   and rings
again
and i wait and i listen and i pray that your smile will make
it over to me

if not today, then maybe tomorrow.

ache:

we search for somewhere safe to be sad
a garden welcoming this shedding skin
our smiles peel back like some past lifetime's paint
where do seven children go when mama goes missing
arms too short
to create home for one another
a seeking septenary, adults aching to heal
without hiding the anger in their hearts
after the anger, there's the pain
is there a guilty God
a sidewalk in Chicago mourning for the mother it claimed
what off brand miracle
what halo-fitted dime bag was handsome enough to charm
a mother away from her children
we do not even speak about yesterday's pain
cannot investigate tomorrow's sorrow
if today has joy
let us have it
unfasten our rib cages and invite every humming bird in
consume the moths hugging this space
this hole where our mother's memory gnaws at us
drains the nectar
caramelizes the calm into cancer
threatens to eradicate the life we have struggled to spit and
stick together
i remember when having a winter coat was a luxury
and food never came on plates but in the form of crumbs
burnt toast
old cheese the color of a light bulb
dimming in and out
inside some poet's bedroom
as he writes
about the dynasty without a daddy

as he writes about how he loves all his siblings but barely
know their favorite color
or the last time they had a good laugh, *together*
where does one go to recover the parts of the soul that
survives the storm
the portion that slips from behind the sepulcher and into the
sea
we need an ocean
to cry into
no church but a cozy couch to fit all of us
say each other's name
sit in a moment to recall that we are blood
and bound by someone who did not love us enough to stay
but we can scramble and find the strength to love beyond
the red lines
the demarcations of addiction
and   breathe   and bless the healing
and the nights we wonder where our mother went maybe
slept, and possibly found *God*

fever dream:

there's enough grief for all of us
to wager a piece of our skin
for the entirety of our survival
a greedy mockery, a gnawing nostalgia
pay the penitence for this private purgatory
our pain pantomimes from glory clothes
marches from our pockets
dances like a swamp
into the offering plate
for what is a church but a chamber where screams go to
learn their names
to learn the tongue of what creates the fire
that created their ash
unraveled a body from a crying mother
a matron mourning
fighting against misogynoir
and praying she is not giving her body to it
giving birth to it
for it is already a war
snatching back your body
from every street corner that makes you criminal
churns your name into a burning wonder
a nigger that found and fashioned some skin and bones to
die in
3/5 human
Entirely a divine death wielder
This is my psalm: Emmett has died a thousand deaths
this is my daily bread: Hope has not forgotten us, here

paint it all black:

paint it all black
the crisp color of your uncle's collarbone
the one who gargles Jim Beam   bronzes the ribs at
family bbqs
each summer as his daddy did
and his daddy's daddy
paint all that shit black   auntie's pound cake   the cups
of Crown   Al Green boomin' in the backyard
fling fingers full of your mother's favorite flower over fetid
fields
where brown bodies are birthed in prayer
silenced in a spray of bullets
within seconds of showing no sign of being armed but in
full possession of blackness
a pasture
where Tupac yells *Young Niggas* on a vintage vinyl and all
the great Spades' partnas got a guaranteed spot in heaven's
ghetto
paint the death black
the weeping boy with the gnashing gold grill   he cracks
a smile, dying on the inside
the mother who hugs her son's memory
he was only 22   his body an equation of bullets, six
carry the two
sounds like the time 16 bullets were sent after Fannie Lou
paint that shit black
the complicit silence
the protests of a pining people
every knot that has lynched the breath from the neck of a
nigga
the juke joints
where gangs and ghosts jive all night long
where a dance goes before the death
where a necrotic paradise is looking for a bed

a home
a willing vessel
and the world shouts
show me your hands
your fro
your frightened but sizzling fists
fox news shouts
show me your skin between the teeth of pitbulls and
alleyways
show us your glory in the hereafter once the knell barks
nigger, nigger
show them your soul and your forgiveness
rap about love
sing about centuries of servitude
make sure you paint all that shit black
so, they'll never forget you have always forgiven them
no matter how many seats are left empty at your dinner
table, as the years pass

take me to the water:

they ask you what you want to be
at this age where bullets are making homes out of all your
friends
you say
      invisible
      free
      a magician
to place your mother's pain in a hat
turn it into a breeze
a forgiving typhoon

these past few months
you have reduced your gusto into gristle
laughed at things just for the sake of surviving   to keep
the nightmares away from your pillow
you have forgotten the joy without the liquor
that a high can exist outside a smoking body
      or blunt

when was the last time your smile and God shared the same
breathing space
school is the boulder in front of the body   the blessing
the books don't do it anymore
these rooms and these floors feel all phantom
unfamiliar
no one in the sky can be proud of this sadness
you and your best friend do not talk as much
the world is unraveling, and you watch it burn in your
favorite pair of blue jeans
that have become too tight, but they are the only thing that
holds you without fear

you are leaving again, quietly on a plane for thirteen hours
headed east

hoping that you will pass over the place that you've been
searching for
a home
a human who loves like a hive   of honey   hiraeth
bones be for the benefit of the family
of the boy shaking inside of you

they ask you where you want to be
when the sun sets and all you can dream to say is
somewhere near water
somewhere baptisms come easy

turn into drops of moonlight:

your back blossoms
each   vertebra   a jeweled cobblestone
calling forth an arrival, a rapture of begging breaths and
shimmering sweat

tender lips tremoring   light as lace
honey tongue massages body into exhale
eyes studded with music   songs that make the body melt
into the sweetest sugar

the soul is not a thing to   be owned   but to be loved then
shared with an equally loving body
easing wars
between the sheets   thighs become places of treaty

feathers fought through heaven's gates
to gaze, *here*
to wander over our bodies   make us fly

soar as we swoon
moan into an oasis
of asking

take me please
give me what you are willing
place your mouth, *here*

unwind your body
lay it down
shake   show your spirit

glow blue

          smile

erupt

        quiver

lips. tender. escorting. heaven. here, oh *here*

a garden for black boys:

i   dream.   cheek-kisses asking away the pain
my mother left
soft   tender soil for my toes to curl into
i know there are bodies here, boys
who have searched Chicago's entire southside for a warm
spot and found nothing but sadness

their eyes arriving fresh, callow cadavers   cop's
collateral
desperately probing for a sanctuary
inside
the dirt
outside the casket

the cankers won't mispronounce their names
the streets mourn these martyrs   but these boys mural
here
watercolor up from polyandriums of lavender
sling their skin back over their bones
eject bullets from holes,   dawn halos   i dream. if the guns
get hungry we leave them starving

hitchhike to a heaven worth their sacrifice
beckoning all my brothers back to me
summoning my sisters
shaking free from the stillness that had them frozen
rising from the crust   curls covered in copper and
stardust

my toes dancing along
lips got a rhyme, an   unforgettable song   to sing
call me Nat King

Lord
this world can be so cold

my hands trembling   pick the sun washed bones up
the polished jewels
forgotten treasures buried
after Birmingham bombings
the bad times everybody kept saying would get better
the hashtags& body bags keep on coming

bad things happen to those who wait too long
too see their mama's baby boy's body
break
bless the healing   the smoking black bodies wrapped in
Gucci sneaks, Gucci tees
the sizzling sisters sought out a savior   pews splintering
the silence sat there and got swallowed

laid away a song to remember
loves it so good she saves herself and her brother
beyond the grave
i watch my friends receive death certificates
before diplomas

fingers full of dirt. tear up the earth
heaven's raining backwards and bringing the bodies
forward
the dinner table is full and there aint no police
the boogie man lost   his badge   and he aint getting it
back
the Lord's dealing with the devilman as we speak

and this garden
this garden is full of blossoming black boys
they know themselves to beautiful,
deserving kings

this garden is full because the graves are empty
the bodies have risen   the kings who perished between
the stages of soil and stardust
they march alongside their lord

saint Emmett all whole and good
as whole as we'll ever be

as whole as we will ever be

i can only belong to myself:

there was a fire and a baptism inside one body
a flood, then an olive branch sprouting like
collard greens in grandma's garden
declaring this skin be free,
belonging only to the bones it has been draped over for 25
years, now

i hang my club clothes and my praying pants
inside the same closet i hid in
tied silence into a special kind of language
rocked it around my white collared shirts

held my flesh to my bones
suffered when love called me out of the darkness
when love called me by the name God knows me by
and i did not have the words to say when i approached the
mirror   guilt steals the voice

cracked my heart open for demagogues
knowing this house be tabernacle
this 5'9 boy be black   as the rifle that threatens the
robber
be black as the earth that swallows the flood
after God has been angry with his children

me loving a snake in the guise of soul mate   air   life
call me yours   i can only belong to myself

i learned the art of melting
into every ocean
into every hymn known to man
i wanted to carry my brokenness   only to the likes that
Christ has felt

and my mother's womb made way for
shaking   breaking   the pressing

this is how you take your body back:

the floor was a dirty wood. the room a closed eyelid. the
door was locked.   i am sure because no one knocked. no
one came through it. someone would have come through it,
right? to see. to stop the fingers from finding things we
teach our bodies to hide. the sweat laid all over my body. i
do not move. i become a clinched fist. a flood braces me
into a thin line of thick questions. is this happening? is this
body mine to give? can a person still live inside the body
after the soul stalls?
i sleep for two decades.
i forget.
i say i forget, aloud.
i aint forgot a thing.
i cry.
i read. i porn. i meet my body for a second time. i explode. i
die. i die. i die.
i high school. i church. i ask god questions. i steel my
clothes. chain my chastity. i religion. i self-blame. i riot. i
forgive. i forgive. forgiveness is the riot.
i survive barely. i fight and wonder what virginity means
for some of us who never got a choice. i don't know the
language of survivors. how do you wear smoke as cologne?
can cologne hide the scent after trauma touches you? it's
been two decades. water bubbles in my lungs.
my dreams flood. the tide rises.
it is not shot in black and white.
full color.
the groping is gray. leaves me confused. i weigh a ton of
feathers.
my smile hides all of this. i think my eyes tell all my
secrets. i still my head.
i am a haunted hue of colors. i bleed begonias.
i tv.
i Oprah.

i hear Maya.
Maya said the rape took her voice for five years.
i see no men.
i hear no men
they say fires like these don't burn black boys. aint i black?
i am black. am i the only one that this has happened to?
i feel alone.

i know i am not.

we take back possession of our bodies when we tell the
truth.

boys bearing names as dark as daffodils:

i asked questions
the kind that makes sex better when you know someone
cares for the condition of your soul
when the kisses truly mean *i love you*
when the heat from our bodies would not laugh us into ash
but dancing flames
into every answer we have ever searched for

to every question that made our bones   feel lonely   or
hollow   or not good enough
or anything that felt too far away from home
and the heavens rejoiced because we never went a day
without praying for one another
a universe where promises do not shatter

days never ended with us knowing anger
but you invited lies into our bed
tucked your secrets underneath   your pillow   held my
hand while doing so

do your lies still ask   about me   do they summon me by
the nicknames you kissed into my throat
the sky does split its skin open when black men burst into
stars
when black men become target practice inside their own
bedrooms

we have no safe place if you cannot love us
without swallowing our names

body smoke:

my friends ask about you
as if your side of the bed still aint on fire
the closet is a furnace that almost killed us both

my cousins still joke about our relationship
trace their fingers over scars they   cannot see   or pay
their weight in rainy nights, with warm meals *to understand*
i swallow the pain in silence

it is all in fun, *right*
they cannot possibly know that black boys with black
sisters can't be strong all the time
we cannot be both the punchline and the applause

the memory of us dangling from the door
& hurting the way we did
making habits and then breaking that shit
as if you were substance to be abused
as if i was just flesh
and wasn't also tired

&
making a mockery of what heaven offers us

i thank the earth that you came,
and left.

for the sake of my soul, thank God you left

ice cream paint job:

the weight of these tears cannot coexist with any fabric
created to wipe my honest invisible
to bear my cross backwards like runaway suicide doors

healing is learning to grieve without your funeral clothes on
without turning every vodka bottle you see
into a sea in which   you drown   baptize   and die again

dub your body celestial being   burgeon into black box
chevy
scoff at the night   ice out the pain   bling away the
bullets
see my chain   even when the lights don't come on
when there isn't a smile or a god to flip the switch

there are days where the sun dries up in my room like some
second-rate lip gloss
my bed, a stomping ground for dreams to rev their engines
my fear-the parking brake
conflagrating around skin that my ancestors prayed for
i sink into myself

> *king on the inside, clean on the outside*
> *smiling on the outside, screaming on the inside*

i ride
i ride

> *king on the inside, clean on the outside*
> *flossing on the outside, empty on the inside*

            i see green fields the color of Harriet's face
deified on twenty-dollar bills
ocean waters the color of tomorrow's best promises

sunrises as pristine as the first day   of creation   aint ever
been rich so i got to celebrate

cover me in an ice cream paint job
candy crayola in the lines for all the black boys outlined
or doing time
for a dime
and the world wants us   to dance   *so we might as well
shine*
name it glory, call it fly
call it free

drive up to heaven in a big rimmed box chevy or grand
marquis

if Hope is the thing with wings, love must be the sky it flies across:

i guess it was the Hope that fed us
plucked bread from behind the jalousie of silence
the slow jams way before SZA was sidestepping niggas
bothering, borrowing her time

skrrt, skrrt
on a song, a psalm that sanctions the dark
cleanses Chicago like Saturday mornings at your mother's
house
the woman that knows nothing about loving her kids but
makes a mean pot of black-eyed peas

maybe it was church mothers praying
tapping the Good Lord on his shoulder,
saying
that's Katherine's boy

and i know my mama wasn't looking for God
but Hopefully she stumbled into him
mentioned me and my siblings' names
all seven of us

maybe it was tears smelling like kerosene
or the beatings that said
tomorrow will be better if you survive today

it was the Hope that saved us
wiped the crumbs from our eyes
pronounced our names responsibly

silver linings do not save us all
drugs do not give a fuck if you ever see your mother alive
again

and drugs don't give a fuck that you're offended by the
word   fuck in this poem
but there is a room tucked away in glory
with your favorite books
and Lauryn Hill singing live   your sister's smile is
framed and hanging on the wall

just in case you are looking to give love a name
and Hope a face

the drought and the famine:

i miss your soul
before the glass got all crazy
turned all shatter
splintered into the kinda days your grandmother's mother
prayed you would make it through
prayed that there would be water in the well when the river
ran dry
or a miracle stored up in somebody's kitchen pantry with
your name on it
i Hope that you are happy
and every day feels like a Pharrell concert because you
deserve unanchored joy
a sun not having to tether the stars
but having the luxury to burn bright,
not for anyone but yourself

the fire you make burns us both:

heaven had a storm
it catcalled us into an anechoic aching
                shhhhhhh
we have not spoken
two mouths dumbed
numbed nebulas kneeling back against back

the sun does not break ground or crown here
we have forfeited our shine
been made blind
resigned from the Divine's design
of who we are and what we were supposed to be

free
aint looked familiar on your face in so long
and maybe my voice reminds you of all the times love
smoked your smile
and left only your bones
i am sorry that *the love* has rubbed you raw

has it got you interrogating your denial
did it answer back
told you that we cannot summon God as if he's some
handmaiden
a cheap magician
parlor tricking your pain into shhhhhhh

silence will break every lie
draw it out of every clay mask you place upon your face
the Potter's hands are lovely, dripping with honey

the salve for your sores
the chamomile for your scraped knees

there's a balm in Broel:

i wear headphones at night
to drown out the symphony of your smile
refusing to hear lips spreading like the last fruit in the forest
unlocking

i numb the shadows of your absence
turning up the volume
even though you are 7,000 miles away

your laugh has been known to make men kneel,
sin, then pray and remember why this day has been given to
us in the first place

your heart has been occupied but never inhabited

who do you let in when the glass sprinkles back into sand
and there's nothing left but you and your anger
who sucks the poison free
who fetches the honey
who prays for your burns when you cannot see them
you are every reminder
that God watches us, his children
even when we are laughing against the stars
the fault
and the glory

when the mirror forgets your name:

you act like you don't remember seeing
your mama kissing the sun
her skin going up yonder   sweat falling
blending into yesterday's rain showers
her body swaying like some breeze searching for a home
eyes fluttering   fingers found some of that stuff
that'll make you lay down your religion
pick up an apology
call it God
or   Hope   too good to be death

boy, you remember when the moon came
told your father it was a perfect night to party
to look at his demons up close
to leave his prayer book   at home   just in case his
children needed to call on the Lord
just in case they needed something to hold onto that refracts
the heat

he went and fell asleep   for good   inside the earth
and you find yourself still waiting patiently for the nap to
end, for a gasp of breath

separating him away from death and the distance between
you

insist upon the glory of your name:

the cognac filled jar
is a boat   is a dream
that stops right before you get to the good part
before you approach the door and see if the promises of
God sit singing

your favorite flowers to life
orchards pop-locking
petals dropping
to your feet

an homage to welcoming your bones home
this soil is the inside joke between your Hope and their fear

love aint ever asked to borrow   your shit   your hand-me-
downs
your transfigured gospels
giving themselves to white men, to beg of them
to pronounce your soul with every gravè and acuté
engraved within its glory

ask them if it is enough
to keep the drowning from kissing you
lend your beginnings to the palm of their hands
and ask for their disjointed amens and hallowed is this
name that "i *will purposely fuck up*

because it sounds too much like king
worthy one
he who writes his pain into gold"
because you are the second chance
coming up from the water

their doubt is the sin you left wading

the cognac filled boat   is a jar full of butterflies
for the nights you cannot summon   your smile   the
darkness will molt into an armada of angels
because even in this, you have loved the lord

and the lord has loved you.

James:

my face is the caricature of a man I know almost nothing
about
if you look close enough   i have my mother's veins

    closer
touch my skin
you will feel my heartbeat is an earthquake

earthquakes oftentimes dress up and pretend they are wars
there are white flags buried underneath this brown skin
maybe yours too

our skin wears loss differently
I cannot seem to remember if i apologized with hugs or
smiles
after telling my father i hated him
for not knowing if my mother would show up this time

blamed him, his precious soul
his tender being
his tired eyes
for all the broken clocks that told the   right time   and my
god, i miss him so much

moon river in oz:

because carefree means
your father came back from the corner store
with butterflies in his veins instead of glass
breaking off inside his blood
dripping honey is the water that runs here
when the food becomes scarce and the prayers don't reach
up to heaven

glory, glory, hallelujah:

every moment be praise
pain prisms itself into color   rainbow rebirth
rattan wrists weave up from under bedsheets
hoping to catch pardon from pillowed prison

stranger calling me by the name I use
to distance myself   from my sin
darkness came and rested
but praise be this heartache
worship be the morning after a one night
stand and having the courage to stand

with your heart in one palm   a prayer in the other
soul be wicker basket bold   I got fruit for days
every moment be   a climax   a celebration
a eulogy
addressed to my former self   a praise

be these bruised bones
breaking, becoming miraculous
and a healing coming up from the earth
gold laid across my tongue

an anthology of Luther Vandross' top hits
hitched   hip-side   New Testaments of black men
prospering
tattooed navicular
meet us at the juke joint   or chapel

we can make this room into   our church   colored boy
synagogue
every moment is a praise

prayer.

whole:

have you ever had to prep a room for your existence
to warn the walls not to crumble into gossip
to send out text messages in advance
saying   i am showing up
all   me   all   male   all him that they do not understand

black and unafraid to love who i love
have you ever had to carve yourself down
in the middle of a conversation
circumventing your truth, too afraid to wear it on your
sleeve

you keep it in your back pocket just in case you forget who
you are tonight
just in case they say the honey you bear is poison
and got all the bees dying
just in case the world tries to wash you into its definition of
clean   of   holy   of being deserving of love

to hell with these boxes and the labels that fall like paper
weights
hold my skin close to yours
do not let another night leave us
without me loving you
without me saying that this moment is all i ever dreamed of

a psalm being cradled by the wind
a storm finding a reason not to rage but to name itself a
wonder
a reckoning
a galaxy full of open arms
of all the things everyone before you told me that i never
deserved

we are God's most   beautiful creations   a syzygy full of
bursting

you make me want to give better hugs
on dark days scaffold the creases in the sky
kiss the moon just to taste the sun's essence
even if i cannot see it
to remind myself, no matter the length of darkness

the dawn will break
find us worthy enough to bless
to be black and full of songs that laugh

you are the reason why the caged bird learned a song
called its friends and family and everyone that wanted to
understand how to love and to be loved
without apology

a place where shame does not have a room
but a powerless name
and joy comes with a smile locked into its teeth
rises to meet us
hemp and ivory plated over its pupils

here, I know your name is a gift
given by God
God has given us a burnishing boy
with a brave smile

the light they found:

we be backpacking backs full of poems
star—stuffed spines shirted up
silencing our secrets from shouting too much noise
collared polos keeping our collarbones quiet
can't let nobody know that this body is full of diamonds
gems your grandmother once wore on her tongue
your mother prayed that your feet would never get too
scared
to start sneaking in your sneakers around your dreams
tiptoeing down the halls of her prayers
with a hurricane lamp in your hands
as if this aint where you are supposed to be
as if this place doesn't deserve a black boy with dreams

oceans touching his feet
kicking off his Giuseppe's
for the gospel
aint the gospel if it doesn't set you free
from labels and any room whose walls feel too much like
tombs
men and women sent to lick the gold off your skin
wring out your smile with both hands
let it dry until you can't even walk back into God's house
or your sister's arms like yall aint kin
or she wasn't your first friend

what is victory but a shame we defeat
a guilt we finally show our bodies to
through the valley of the shadow of death
we shall fear no evil or heartbreak
only our gold turning into dust
without the sun knowing our names and the hoods we came
from
knowing that we are God's children

but that boy has a black mother
and he is his father's only son

all the lights, the flashing lights:

but aren't we all just searching for somewhere safe enough
to walk barefoot
eyes not searching
for shattered glass   hungry bullets   cautions signs
ears having to unravel against the night
to hear the sizzling pop of the streetlight breathing on

buzzing for the bugs to come
to make a meeting place out of our skin
unfurl it into a blanket   a   nest   a high-rise
pleading for demolition

an implosion of bone and Hope
we pray for rooms that do not swallow us
churches whose god is not angry all the time when our
arms sometimes fall to our sides
in a sigh or ungrateful silence

we know that our grins can only lift so much of the guilt
but is it wrong to want to belong to yourself
to keep the last of your parts sacred
before everything about you becomes   confetti   a
show   a flake of plastic
a mud statue always melting and being made and shaped
without ever becoming that in which you truly are

tell me
is it wrong to store the last of the butterflies inside of your
throat
to keep beautiful things within you
for fear of absolute freedom   destruction
becoming the buzzing pop inside the street lamp

this is for every brown and black woman and man that
never made it home before the streets came on

a haiku:

these burials are not autobiographical
but they still belong to me

azaleas drinking pale moonbeams *after Frank Ocean*:

whoever you are. wherever you are… i'm starting to think
we're a lot alike

      i have watched what they do to men
      who saunter like sheep

the wolves howl
huddle around the leper as if he's a deck of cards
his existence is a constant reneging in a game of spades
the boy's blood smells too much of spring showers

his mother's perfume stamps x's over his wrists
somersaulting her son's spine into a standing spray

whoever you are. wherever you are… i'm starting to think
we're a lot alike

he fights himself   even titans marvel and bow at the
mechanics of machismo

      the wolves gaze   *all wanting to be seen, touched,*
heard, paid attention to

he cannot scratch the buds out of his blood quick enough
the bleeding hearts' tangle his beard   rumbles out of the
quiet   spills over the ledge of his lips
he reaches for anyone's daughter
fills his pants with women who will teach
their daughters to nestle razor blades underneath their
tongues
for the moment masculinity becomes a breast bone

carved into a bowl

demanding from even the meekness of sheep to leave its
name at home, *in the closet*

*whoever you are. wherever you are…i'm starting to think
we're a lot alike*

        teeth razor the safety gone
        ready to tear sweetness out of someone's
son
        there must be for life's sake, a howl
hibernating inside his high pitch hums

      i see what the village does when the choir boys go
quiet
      the congregation exacts the voices but never the
bodies

the boy closes his eyes   the moon falls, forgets its place

      i don't have any secrets i need kept anymore
      there are no howling wolves

*i feel like a free man. if i listen closely… i can hear the sky
falling too*

more than the stars in the sky:

stretch your arms wide
palms skyward
until every ocean you have imbibed pours forth
set dynamite to the levees

bow down before God
demand   forgiveness   the mirror will not splinter
there will be a breaking before the blessing
a dampening of skin

freedom demands sweat and a song we know all the words
to
Lauryn Hill's, I Find It Hard to Say
love aint got a bedroom but a church
an   altar   where the baptisms don't drown you

bullets and bombs are circumcised into ash
when trying to penetrate the stained-glass windows
and no one cares if you smell like last   night's weed   or
tomorrow's eulogy
we all tryin' to make it into heaven

hand in hand
with some glow on our skin
and maybe if we are lucky, even
a smile across our lips

acknowledgments

i cannot say thank you enough to the following publications in which my poems appear in some form.

Meniscus Literary Journal, "Dancing on the Moon"

Spiral Orb, "When the Saints Go Marching They Bring Their Sisters"

Connotation Press, "God Whispers Him up from That Grief"

Scalawag Magazine, "Body Smoke".

Obsidian Magazine, "Triptych" and "Boys Bearing Names as Dark as Daffodils"

Thank you to all my family, friends, and peers. You make me better. You allow me to be brave.

None of this would have been possible without the women in my life who steadily show me that love is the most liberating and reckoning force. You show me God's face.

For my brothers of blood and of loyalty. The iron is still sharp.

Eleanor, it remains serendipity indeed.

Vicki Leak---thoughts of a brighter future blossomed in your office. To you, I am grateful.

Phyllis Lockhart, there are not enough days left in this life or the next to say thank you for everything you do.

Lanita Douglas, you are an example of what selflessness is. I sincerely appreciate your life and love. My poetry found its breath under your roof.

Faye Abner, I have not forgotten the love given. This is for *you.*

With a special mention to: Dr. Lakerri Mack, Ashley Gilomen (Mama G), Julie Stewart, Jametta Clarke, Andrew Leak, Dayle Cook, Debra Clark, Deborah Hicks, Dana Williford, Shantel Barginere, Geneva Wilson and the various educators I have encountered across the years, thank you for sowing into this *soil.*

Jamillah, Hannah, Zeph--- you make me better. Thank you for your creative ingenuity, your swelling hearts and dedication to this work.

Kelsey, you are my person. Everyone deserves a friend like you. Thank you for listening to my ideas and encouraging my art. Always.

about the author

W.J. Lofton is an artist, poet, and activist residing in Atlanta, GA. *A Garden for Black Boys* is his sophomore collection, continuing his campaign on healing and equity for black people. He is also the author of *These Flowers were held by Broken Vases*, published in 2016. His poetry reflects his experiences and those around him. He is a Chicago native, yet has spent most of his young adulthood living in the south. Lofton hopes to leave a legacy centered on a collective healing through his activism and art. You can stay in contact with the writer at thepoetschair.com and interact with him on social media via his Instagram page, @mrjamespoetry.

Made in the USA
Columbia, SC
15 February 2020

87989492R00040